AUP
new
poets
10

Tessa Keenan
romesh dissanayake
Sadie Lawrence

Edited and with a foreword
by Anne Kennedy

T0272415

AUCKLAND
UNIVERSITY
PRESS

Contents

romesh dissanayake
Favourite Flavour House

Sadie Lawrence

Like Human Girls /all we have is noise

Foreword

AUP New Poets 10 presents three young poets whose respective
voices stand out for their persuasive power and newness.
These poets explore vital themes such as identity, history,
perception, love and loss. Each poet writes, in different ways,
a compelling present. At the same time, they bring knowledge
of their own heritage with them – along with their inheritance
of poetic form. Each understands how poetry, with its
freedoms and shapes, its inventions and borrowings, reaches
out. The fresh voices of *New Poets 10* have produced urgent
work that allows us to perceive our contemporary world in
ways we would not have otherwise.

Tessa Keenan (Te Ātiawa) looks out from the raw now at
a landscape peopled with her tūpuna, and her poems form
a kind of bridge between those realities. A room filled with
fan heaters, fitted sheets and strange novels is also 'a room
where we cannot remember the memories we made a room
a room a self-portrait'. Keenan juxtaposes the new and the
old with rising emotion, from 'These days we are a photograph;
/ one of a farm / strewn with cows that used to be / bright
harakeke or swamp' to the final aching sequence 'Some Other
Pā'. These poems have no tidy resolution; they delve into the
past, notice collisions, ask questions. Throughout, Keenan's ear
for the music of language smuggles in a quiet and essential rage.

romesh dissanayake makes daring language collages to explore
his early years in post-war Sri Lanka and his adult life in
Aotearoa. With playful use of sound, space, narrative and self-
reflexivity, the poet tells it how it is: 'we can do what we damn
please / because this is our poem / about being on holiday'.
These poems are never still. Compelling images of food and
family give way to edgy romance, unsettling moments and
tongue-in-cheek references: 'eating a peach in the sun I wonder'.

dissanayake is a poet whose voice is assured yet original, aching yet hopeful, experimental yet direct: 'i've been telling jobseekers soften your language / so that your name   all fleshy and ripe / doesn't set off any alarms'.

Sadie Lawrence's poems concern the anguish of rite-of-passage in a complicated world, yet in the end their inventiveness and beauty deliver hope. These poems don't flinch from first love, bullying, nosebleeds. Vocally, a rich formality is juxtaposed with playfulness: 'The chicken-wire woodwork engraves my knees / and you are one jacket poorer, enduring the chill.' Metaphors and similes are frequent and searing: 'love took me in its jaws / like a weary old dog'. Settings are often stark with a suburban-Gothic tinge applied to locations such as a bridge at night, a laundromat, a two-bedroom flat. Lawrence's poetic *roman à clef* is complex, daring and tough with self-awareness: 'thank you, but / I've already had my baptism' ('Ode to the Autism Diagnosis Report').

Anne Kennedy

Tessa Keenan

Pukapuka mapi / Atlas

A Room Recording

A room a room a fan heater socketed to the wall placed a ruler's length away
from any wooden surface a room for dusted carpet and a camera socketed
to a computer and footprints a room where love was made and wraps
were made the night before a room to get out of bed if the house was still
standing in the morning it would throw its chin to the maunga with a room
full of pride a room fitted sheets folded wonky socketed to the cupboard
a room a room a bunker to play world war one and fight over the phone
a room coming back to us in ways we cannot explain except that we are
compelled to a room to listen to the smashing pumpkins in a room a room
alone with a video camera on talking to a room full of strange novels strange
lego strange history a room and an active volcano a room that becomes
simultaneously a room and not a room when it is bragged about live on the
internet an old vacuum a room unrecognisable from a room it used to be a
room a room a take-your-clothes-off-when-it-is-too-warm instruction but
stick uncomfortably with sunblock and residue of a room full of skin locked
inside itself a room where we cannot remember the memories we made a
room a room a self-portrait.

A World of Perpetual Longing

It looks like they touch when the cloud comes in and coats the mountains, I know. This is what Tāwh wants you to believe. It's actually just a curtain.

Think: holding a friend's towel up in front of them while they get dressed after swimming.

Think further: a steeple doesn't leave behind anything that would need tweezing out. Some days the ground freezes over and it is the sun that eventually warms it. New species get names, conservationists increase the population of kākāpō, buildings are assembled then moved on the back of trucks. There has to be space, something to stand on, and something to reach for. As a consequence, this is a world of perpetual longing. Nothing can be said without breathing in thousands of years of desire. When you tell me how you are happy to be home, and how when you were a kid you escaped to the beach, running over grass to dodge the prickles then running over sand to shorten the burn, your words are born from the thoughts of those who longed for that before you.

Think further again: the sky was bland at the bus station. I stood outside and waited for you to find a seat, yelled 'Bye!' when you did.

On my way home, I thought about the night before: climbing over you as you sweated, reaching along the walls with eyes unblinking, trying to find the light switch, your hands drawing dreams of lakes, wheels, and winds on my skin as you slept, the last thing you whispered before falling asleep. By the time you got to Whanganui it was blue as summer and the trees stretched as if it was morning. They were so close to touching. I sat there breathing and breathing.

Mātou

These days we are a photograph;
one of a farm
strewn with cows that used to be
bright harakeke or swamp.

The kids point at it
and say the sun sits
behind a smudge (left by
someone at Christmas);
the water turned hot that day:
in the bottom right-hand corner,
a trough sparkles
to prove it.

Across the fields there is a mountain.
Beyond that, the city we live in.

(We were driving up a road we'd never been on
when Dad told Mum to stop.

He opened the car door
and walked up to a nearby fence.

I don't know what,
or who, told him
he was in the right place:
the weight of trying to remember
often gets you lost

but he pointed at the grass, turned back to us,
and yelled
'this is your tupuna!')

Ōākura Beach

That space asks for something to enter it.
I imagine people walking with clean washing
towards the sea.

Sheets are coloured by the sky's reflection.
Children dragging sticks behind them,
faced with distance,
flatten the sand's wind-blown lips.

This is the first day of my lonely spell.
Seagulls are locked above like cut-outs.

There is nobody around, really. Extinction
is the only thing on the beach.

The wind tucks its fingers into the space
between an ocean and a home.
I see it slide through the people I've imagined.
It whispers an imperative.

Postcard

There was a parking ticket tucked under my windscreen wiper today.
    'Fuck,'   I might've said to you.

    You wouldn't tell me to calm down. You don't drive
    and don't know that parking tickets are only $12 in the regions.

I plucked it out and put it into my book.

    Replacing a boarding pass.

I went for a swim in the river. A house is for sale across the road where I usually
park. It is grey in all the wrong places. The trimming around the deck is paisley.

    I used to drive past it every week, sitting behind the driver's seat on the
    way to swimming lessons and I didn't even notice it. Now I run past the
    house on my lunch breaks, plotting how to pay for a flight to you and
    how to remember to send you the postcard crumpled at the bottom of
    my bag.

On the phone last night, it sounded like you were sketching. Was it the washing
machine at your uncle's?

    You were drawing me, or maybe some fruit. The water is always cold
    where you are and it's good to draw summer fruits for something warm
    to do.

It's weird. All the songs I've begun to like mention rivers running out to the ocean.

    I might've sung them to you.

On hot days, I get into my car and the steering wheel burns me like black sand.

    I wait for your postcard. It flies over these bodies of water.

Coastal Driveway Song

In your car / I am recording the best bathroom stall conversation / and it starts with pressing your foot to the accelerator / like make an echo noise which means whisper / then wait / put your wrists together and push the noise forward / we will generate unexpected steam / making the buttons tremble and tearing you up / like an odd look / odd ponytails / you driving a mini / I want to spend my money on microphones / to attach to every corner of your car / in some ways / we are fake / we can try to make background noise drive us to a garden of sweaty men who like neo-funk / our ankles / our tape / our restricted licences / I hated noise before we started / now I want to take it / I like the way your hips look / moving / pretending they're not belted to a seat.

Scurvy Girls

In the middle of a lecture about climate change and the Suez Canal,
Sophie realised she must be a pirate.

Since Kate stopped eating dinner, she has become limp and wilted.
She bends around the room slowly.
      She hopes her touch won't interrupt the wooden floor.

Runa wears a black buckled corset over a white shirt to a glow-in-the-dark party,
so it looks like she doesn't have a heart.

'When I stand up for too long, my legs are not attached to my body at all,'
      thinks Bridget.
'They don't even resemble wooden legs or a mermaid tail.'

Tanya goes home for the holidays. Malt and chocolate end up down her top.
Her mum is a good baker. She flies their flag at half-mast.

Gemma vomits millions of squished orange and green gummy fish
      into an Aro Street gutter
on the way home from her boyfriend's.

A woman in the house across the road turns her lights on
      once Phaedra shuts her curtains.
Her body emanates a yellow glow. It calms with the night and the sea.

When Janhavi is embarrassed about spending money she orders a filter coffee.
There is a small person inside her that enjoys watery things.

Our ship is sinking
and I haven't bought any fruit.

Celesta

All this talk about rovers and
  breakthroughs has got me thinking,
   churning through, in a way, how,
    despite making me want to drive straight into my
     elderly neighbour's front door, there's a sort of
     finesse about the way you conduct me and
      gravitate my eyes towards the black hole connecting your
     heart and left nipple, like some marionette, some
     indecent beautifier ignorantly inspired by
      just the mere memory of our first
      kiss under planetary alignment,
       lifting off the fact that you didn't even know
        me, in a way, and forgot I'd acknowledged you on that
         night when I noticed the twist of your ankles the second they lifted
        off the grass and how the curve of your back is the tide's
       pull but with blackheads and a permanently
       quizzical frown. Look, we are small, and we
      rarely have control over what we
      say around each other, but all this
       talk comes out anyway because
        underneath it's just you and the stars pretending to be
        Venus, giving me routine desire to
        watch you orbit me and put an
         x where I think my thoughts are born or
        young within myself, and not a result of you.

What You Will Do

When you come to my house there will be pieces of hay under my windowsill
or are they skin and I will play records you will come and have a look at my
mugs in my house when I get ready for you I put my red shoes in a wicker
basket and watch them shrink while I wrap my wet hair in a towel I like to
walk around naked before you come to me and for me and not feel anything
drop or sway I move my arms before pulling on a shirt when you come in
you come to my red kettle it boils and doesn't ever stop because the button
is broken you will watch everything I do I will trace the outline of the old
landline while I stand in front of you and stand in my bedroom and wait for
your call even though you are there I wish I could wrap a tight cord around
my fingers and yours when we shower I like to drip dry making tiny paths on
the floor that fade in the fake sun coming through the hand-printed windows
the air will touch me more than cotton and I hope you don't mind and I hope
you help keep me soft my elbows are pointy and my knees bend to the music
I will make you do the same when you listen to my records when we break
our dancing I will go to the bathroom and put my nose against the mirror tilt
my head up and look myself in the eyes so I am beyond tough for you I come
back and say stay right there stay right there you look good in that light and
you will not agree but this is my house and I get to tell you what you will do
and feel or do I?

Permission to Hate

I stole your perfect shirt. I hate that it has no holes in it.
Like I hate ownership   and I hate money   and I hate colonisation.

I used to be afraid to play piano for my family.
But I learnt to deal with it.   I learnt
an easy song to fill a room with performative joy and to do what I was asked.
I was awful and I wanted to die when they clapped.

I used to be neat and tidy like I was at a Swiss finishing school
        and I hated it.
The silence and order sewed me so tight.
I wore a tie to prove my shirts were in order
        when really they were all over my floor.

Now I'm holey and hating everything. See:
colonisation,   money,   ownership.
I own my hatred. The fire burns full circles out of your fabric.

Tell me, for the sake of my own voyeuristic interests.
When I give it back to you, will you ever rip up your shirt and hate?

I don't care if it will be
for the sake of fashion or   for the sake of holes or
        for the sake of growth.
You are allowed to hate the way it is.

Killing Time at the Canterbury Museum
after Ana Iti

The whare is deserted. I sit
a little way back from the glass. A dad
points at where a fire was lit

while his kid eats a muesli bar. This exhibit has no
mannequins. I'm surprised, but glad
about it. At the gallery yesterday, I watched an artist sit

in front of this exhibit in a film that played on a loop.
There used to be mannequins crouching low on the sand.
One of them had meat to hang above a fire they lit.

In another display, mannequins sat in a cave as the hills burned.
Some looked down, hunched over knees, naked. As
though all our people did back then was sit and sit.

Now it's different. Just a lot of empty space.
The cave is still there, clad
with burns from where a fire was lit.

I say, 'Something's missing.'
My dad agrees and checks his watch. We're both relieved that
we only have thirty minutes left to sit
in the next room, about Antarctic explorers, and learn (if we want)
where their fires were lit.

Tataraimaka Pā

I take the sandwich
from the wrap
and eat the currants.
You stand, back against the pā,
where your tūpuna rot
with flu.

It reminds me of forgetting.
Or missing a dentist appointment.

This could pass
for a dreary picnic.
I can barely see the pā,
the flush in your cheeks,
and the black shroud on the mountain.

Your Honda
parked by the sea
looks like an aggressor.

The gravel mutters.
Muskets and headless bodies mutter.
Last night the TV muttered 'southerlies'.

We are clutching at food
and crying because we know
we are the only ones that know.

Through Matekai Park

When biking through the park, its name
makes me think of fruit
being pulled from a tree.
Or Mr Minister,
my primary school teacher,
and his love of moko mangaeka.
Then I remember the girl,
five years younger than me,
waving at me in the park
during lockdown.
M told me, 'She's got a girlfriend too.'
In 2013 we blindfolded S
on their last day at school.
We took them down the clay
over the bridge
over the swamp
over the gravel,
and said we will miss them.
My friend's garden backs onto the park.
Another's friend's dad buried a pot of jelly
snakes by the little wooden bridge.
We used to find a tyre swing
through the mud.
Now we find it's not there.

D's on a single speed in front of me.
I haven't worn sunglasses
I'm crying from the dirt.
Someone's chocolate Lab comes in and
out of the bushes.
I slow down before I reach
the next corner,
expecting an owner.
I gather a lot of speed
by the time we reach the hill.
D weaves around the wooden post
and stretches up first.
Once we come out
we ride down the main road
to the campsite.
At the campsite, the Christian Surfers
are having their annual gathering.
Their band is playing Tash Sultana.
I try and fail to jump over a speed bump.
A husband, wife and child stand aside
and let us pass.
Then we bike past Mr Minister.

Moonwalk

I am an okay dancer, but tonight I am a woman walking home
      And I am looking at the moon.
It is waxing gibbous.
      My period is due in the new moon. I still have time.

I know there's a great distance between the earth and other things in space,
      Like there is between me and my unmade bed right now.
I didn't have time to make it this morning.
The kākā and my phone distracted me.

On this walk, I have time to look at the moon among other bright things.
      A hotel sign, the concrete before my shadow hits it. Cars.

One day I will run out of new things to do.
      I hope there will still be things to look at without distraction.

Then I will be able to put more time into my appearance and my room.
I will practise moonwalking again.
I will have time to travel greater distances and look up.

Te Aro

If you're in the city, looking for her,   the girl that will bring you
back to yourself,   here's my advice:
keep your back straight, head up, and eyes to the shuffling horizon.
Every tree is supposed to tower that way   to the right
anchored left   slowly rotting.
You blink and it is the next day. Black   is green again.
Light is peeling back bushes and showing you something you knew.
It won't be her.   But
in a way that requires you to anticipate,   fighting the summer air,
there's a place where her house could be. It's not actually her house,
but you will,   after you let yourself love her,
go there again and again   to ask Te Aro why
the street is so steep,   bushes bend, kākā circle, and
you were so silly to think it was. Then, you're doing it right.   Every
house could be hers. It's exciting, never ending.   Keep looking,
as I said, you're being stupid and deluded   but
you're going to find her.

Taranaki

Trenches look like
the ground's small intestine
cut in half.
Arising and digesting.

I thought of my ancestors' bodies.

It was hard to get up.
The wind slurped the curtains
out of the glass.

I crouched towards my stomach.
And it rained for ages.
Leaves turned to mush in the gutter.

I felt my intolerance
of yesterday's two-dollar
Mitre 10 sausage.

A family member
lying horizontal
in the grass outside

said:
'In a trench
you're half buried.'

Some Other Pā

I've been told to map myself.

Mapping isn't something you can do in stillness. My ancestors moved their mouths and bodies to their families, and their families moved their mouths and bodies to their new families. In notes irreplicable in European music, they mapped their journeys.

I grew up fifteen minutes' drive from the islands where my ancestors' children fished, swam, threw tantrums, cuddled each other, and died. Fifteen minutes' drive from the urupā with thousands of unmarked graves. My nana is buried in a marked one, near her nana.

I grew up on land that, based on modern maps, is just outside that which I have an ancestral connection to. There's a bit of debated crossover between the towns where the land belongs to both, says Te Puni Kōkiri. When you step outside it you're in the wrong zone.

We were welcome at the marae down the hill from our house because of our ancestor marrying a local ancestor, and that was the end of a war. My dad sat on the pae during school marae visits. One map sets vastly different rules from the other.

I have to map myself.

My other ancestors knew their destination from a page. They mapped out their homes, piece of wood by piece of wood, then road by road. The land would let them, and it did. It was bare, volcanic, wet, rugged.

I map myself.

Even when I'm my stillest, I'm always running between two towns, two maps. We are people in motion now. We go towards and away from every home.

At the site of every battle is a home or stockade. There are so many of them along
every road I travel, some screamingly visible, some only so by plane or Google
Earth. I am in motion, running past these when thinking about who I am.

I get up,
      leave my house,
            throw my arms in the air,
                  open my mouth,
                        and sing to all of the land I know.

When this survey is done, I get to writing about pā.

1.　Puke Ariki

You know this one. Picture it.
　　　People sit next to the river

and I don't know why.
　　　It's dirty with food wrappers.

One of its banks is a parking lot.
　　　If you turn around,

there's a museum to look at.
　　　It might have a good exhibition.

Maybe we can't stop
　　　coming back to where we can sit and know nothing, and that is okay.

Maybe we are always coming back
　　　to the water.

2. Ōtaka

When I go to the urupā on a sunny day
I bring my UE Boom
and play 'Love Is Just a Four-Letter Word'.
Or I bring some old, wooden knitting needles.

3.   Te Ngahoro

There's a sign for it, but
who has driven down this road?
Constabulary?
Cross-country runners?
The person who put up
Harold the Giraffe?
Kids are asking me
when I drive them into town.
I don't know what to say.
Where's Harold's owner?
Who lives here?
I want to ask:
Why is there a road?
Who *lived* here? And
where did they go
when they fell?

4.   Omuna

We can be here
        through marriage, somehow,
               or private land purchase next door.
      We wave Mr Whippy down
the marae driveway.
The cousins take their ice creams
      down to the river. Nana
          looks across it

and up.

5. Pahitere

Pahitere has been there the longest,
at least from your perspective.

It's a million-dollar pā. There's a million-dollar
school up the road now.

You think you dreamt this pā up, next to
strawberries, farm tanks, and bulls.

But every time you go home, it's there.

You couldn't hide from it if you tried,
and maybe that is a reminder.

You should be here, and here you are.
What are you going to do about it?

romesh dissanayake

Favourite Flavour House

Pandan for dosa
for Marlar

—

Jean's only open wed to sun and
sells out in the mornings
But that's Upper Hutt not Lower
Hutt
Nature Vege nori fried rice, wonton
noodle black bean sauce, crispy
soy nuggets
Han River everything
Swad for set lunch trays, samosa
chaat, bhel pav
Jean's does do mean savoury
pastries
Brewtown Sunday market also for
Ethiopia feed

—

The Mumma

About six months ago our fish supplier, Aravinda – who's the only one who goes out past the rocks in Wainui and gets us gooseneck barnacles when we ask for them, yes, that Aravinda – called us up and said he'd caught the big one.

I thought he meant kingfish. The sea spray in his soaked beard muffled his voice and made it damn near impossible to tell what the hell he was on about. He said he'd caught the One. The big one he'd been talking about for ages.
Craaayfish. Not kingfish. *Crayfish*!
The Mumma.

The way he carted her in mid-service through the dining room dripping made it seem like it was the theatre. And the diners were scene-setting props. And we were the audience. Because Aravinda commands that kind of attention when he walks into a room.

He plopped the Mumma on Danae's pastry bench and we all gathered around – eyes wide, tongues out. Srinidhi had the great idea to keep her alive for a week so that Indika could see the Mumma when she got back from her holiday back home. Jing-wen said that her grandfather could get us seaweed from Seatoun because, he knew, that's what the Mumma likes to eat.

Well, when Indika got back from her holiday a week later, all moisturised and glowing, she said she couldn't do it. And Raquel said she couldn't do it either. And neither could Amelia, or Kasey . . . And there was no way in hell I would miss out on an opportunity to bring the kitchen team closer together, so I said I couldn't do it either.

That was about six months ago and the truth is, Mum is still here. She looks after us and cares for us and really, we love her.

Each time Aravinda comes in with his big gleamy eyes, his glistening beard, his bloody splintered fingernails and asks us about her, we all hide in the walk-in and say, yesss, she was so tasty, Aravinda.

We say, mmmm you're such a good fisher-man, Aravinda.

B.A.D.D.I.E.S.

B oldly going where no sea slug has gone before.

A dding lots of sauce, not even caring if it gets on your shirt.

D id I ever tell you about the time Mikaere got into the club with no shoes on?

D on't even dare mention dimensions when you're talking about me.

I t's a matter of passing things down with two hands to your elders.

E xactly what I mean. A perfect example.

S lipping away. Baddies be. Too bad for you.

Tay has stans

but someone called me fruity this morning and i
spent the next three hours writing
a shopping list
for a store which doesn't exist yet

that's what poetry means to me

and my poems are a dropped wallet
by which i mean, cashless
by which i mean, filled with pictures of family
by which i mean, cashless

think of every line you've ever sat on
every time you've sat to shit
every tyre-kicking foreign ending
stanky, roachy, chuckling

well-worn slipper lips
donut sugar lips
a tortoise breakdancing breakneck
backspinning

that's what poetry means to me

look at my wee tomato plant
standing tippy-toe on top of a terracotta mortar
it's ripe red, dangling red
how can i speak of how fruity it is
without speaking of the flimsy furry white stem
that i once nearly drowned

Two gentle strangers

when i took the වම් පැත්ත turn-off on state highway 1
i forgot to take my нога off the 브레이크 pedal and
i slid for what seemed like වසර
into what seemed like
another время
another යුගය, another 세계
where
사람들   люди   මිනිසුන්
were all standing by the bypass and
болеть for me.

even though it was страшный
i was wasn't ලැජ්ජයි about it.

i met my crystal дворец

finally.

Six a.m. in Colombo / Cinnamon Gardens

5

on the way to colombo 7
cinnamon gardens
holding back vomit on the school van
because   *the heat*
because   the coconut oil in the boy's hair next to me has long gone rancid

the driver points the aircon in my direction and checks the air
flow with his hand

i saw a boy get a 1 m wooden ruler snapped over his head
because he spelled cat with a 'k'

i saw a komodo dragon's tongue slithering through the grass
i was supine staring up at the sun wishing the clouds
weren't so far away

i was run over by that same van   by that same driver
right outside that   same school
my bag snagged on the axle
the driver pinched the brakes, panicked   sped off

we were both thinking of our families

7

we use mosquito nets as repellent
and count the money under our mattresses
we are   planning our escape

the same time we won the cricket world cup in '96
the same time murali was called for chucking
the same time arjuna ranatunga's full belly
scampered between wickets
the same time we blew up villages up north
to lentil proportions

they played billy ocean's *when the going gets tough,*
the tough get going
over a montage of the best shots from the final
a victory lap
but when the going gets tough   the educated emigrate
and when the going got rough
we sold wood apple juice
sealed in small plastic tubes
with a comb and a candle
and bought three
wet summers' worth in airfares

12

mum enters a competition on the back of a laundry powder box
i win a game boy and pokémon   blue

i collect the rubber skins inside of coke bottle tops
under the bleachers at school sports day in newtown
sixteen more and i'll have a new alcatel phone

all my friends are asleep so i text random numbers at night
under the covers
asking them if they've got the time

14

i once saw my science teacher   who was also a brother
throw a piece of chalk at hayden in the back of the class

neither of them asked for forgiveness
because it was such a good shot

17

my sister is christened and her christian name is now *mary*
my science teacher   who is also a brother
is also her godfather
each year he sends her a postcard
with nothing inside it

19

i am driving a white girl home on christmas eve at four in the morning
her bike's in the boot
the beers i've had and the joint that got passed around
in the back of my mind

when a police car pulls us over
they don't breath test me
or let me explain why   i'm on my restricted
why my seat belt isn't on
why my front bumper is dangling

23

please lord let me be a humble skuxx
drafting instagram posts on the plane

24

in london on boxing day coked up   coked out
the part of me which i thought i knew
went straight through a fence
straight through the strait of gibraltar
i was sick of the sea

i was someone's tinder date who fell through
i was all skinny jeans and trucker hats
i tell people i've only been sunburnt once in my life
to prove that brown people on tour are pretty much fearless

29
it's okay to stay up past midnight
because i've only got two meetings in the morning
and one of them is online
and the other is with myself

and the corn should be ready   stardew valley
and the cows need milking too
and i'm married and have   two biracial children
zooming around pelican town on my horse
i give gifts to the villagers

it's not money that's important in this life
but gifts – gifts and tasks are important
not money
i just go around handing out gifts
collecting my corn
completing my little tasks

the way i'm used to describing my
self-changing

34
i buried *when i open the shop*
next to babula and ded's grave
then washed the bird poop off the bench we   the loving living
sanded and varnished
one christmas

it hurts to remember
i've been putting this trip off for so long

i'm no good at keeping people alive
after they've gone

especially when they
passed in service of me

To find your heroes are shit dancers
for Jerry ~ R.I.P. Legend

Jerry Collins once came to our school
got up at assembly
and talked to us about how we should
stay in class and do our work

Whatta bots guy, Jerry
what did he know of

how we had to glow up in the dark
a celestial luminescence
kiribath dreams

had to do push-ups in the bathtub
while sounding out vowels

They tried to scare us with all sorts of
age-old cheese-like
middle-aged smelly-breath
soccer-coach tricks

Half-caste, my arse

While I knew four languages once
three of them were the white man's

Let me tell you about how i trojan-horsed my chink eyes
among the obedient and polite
how i crept out under a waning moon
and lassoed your dreams

To find your heroes are shit dancers
while my braided tassels
dripping, swing free

Walnuts

hui brings me dried plums and walnuts from his orchard. I am reading his
ghost stories in waikanae. the tea he brings me smells of buddhist monasteries
... of sand impressions and crumbling incense. generosity surrounds me here.
there is no pretence, no holes within the silence, no mumbling ... a rarity for
a ruffian like me ... a head full of clutter.

- there is an air of confrontation about my mother that neither i, nor
  she, cares to address.
- there is a bold bull on the grass and feeble cotton on the clothesline.
- there are things to be said about clarity which cannot be suffused with
  catch-all euphemisms.

hui brings me half-cracked walnuts from his orchard and as I break them
even further, crushing them between my thumbs, they break like, well,
walnut shells – what else did you expect?

except ...
i expect my body to break like they break
i expect power structures to crumble upon my return
i expect to set free all the anger shielding my shame
i expect to set free all the guilt i thought i had made
i expect to set free babula's pelmeni
so that she knows she didn't die in vain
i expect to set free all these identities living within me
to my brothers, to my sisters,
to my job seekers
i'm serious
what is this, if not
how we break a few shells

Favourite Flavour House

When i walk out of my office and into the kitchen i see   Indika holding
a courgette between her legs and   Kasey laughing, on her knees,
pretending to suck on it as   Srinidhi shakes her head as   Raquel pours
parsnip stock from a 30 L pot on the stove through a paper fat-filter into
a plastic bucket on the floor as   Duncan swipes the leftover food from
the plates that come back with the side of his palm into a hole in the bench
as   Bianca drops a napkin on the floor in front of him on accident on
purpose   as the door from the walk-in slides open and   Amelia
emerges with a tray of truffle raviolo in one hand and   a container of
cut kūmara and imitation caviar inside of a carton of eggs in the other
as   Mickee unties her denim FOH apron and   pulls out a pack
of cigarettes from the front pocket of her waistcoat and   heads to
the rubbish bin rooms as   Jing-wen reaches on tip-toe for her sugar
thermometer inside of her knife roll at the top of the pantry as   a pan
of darkening caramel sizzles behind her as   Grayson bends over the
deep fryer with a dripping Steelo in his hand next   to a 4 L plastic
container of soapy water next   to the flat-top   next to the pasta
blancher   next to the docket machine whirring tickets   creating its
own currents   next to the pass   next to the unpacked vege delivery
box   next to the front door of my office and i think   how is this still
my favourite flavour house

Halloween

K just managed to split the quarter tab. so what's that? i just put the
   most wellington thing in my coffee. sun in the sky, you know
   how i feel.

an eighth arriving.

Aunties in high-vis patrol the north and south entrance to
   marukaikuru. the developers came yesterday and the food tent
   was moved to the back. there are ladies in jogging gear who wave
   as they go past and rubbish truck drivers toot-toot their horns.

it's all good for now but

who's turning up next?

J just wrapped the smoke alarm in a clean tea towel and shoved it in
   the freezer again. has set off a borer bomb in the house again. he
   munches on pork crackling, shattering walls, and tells P, as she's
   looking for a sleeping bag behind the TV in the living room, that
   she can't stay for the night.

who am i to get in the way of a sunken revolution?

N was blowing bubbles on the balcony. she went to pick her negroni
   up from off the floor and the fold-out chair from last camping
   weekend caved in on itself. don't take this the wrong way but the
   way the setting sun crept under the parapet reminded me of san
   francisco, and i could have stayed there forever, if it wasn't for
   the drip, drip-dripping and the bag of frozen peas. and the way
   that her jaw swelled and dislocated.

by nightfall.

I saw D cough up his spirit. beetroot soup all down the walls. scratch
        that, i won't go there. bounce it off the backboard.

Toilet paper drips from the ceiling like stalactites in dimly lit caves.
        the bouncer outside 121 with a missing eye and 'best before'
        tattooed on his neck, lifted me up off the ground and i couldn't
        summon enough slime to slither away.

Dream 4:46 a.m., novel idea?

In the quiet din of the hospital waiting room. the mosquitos surfing
        the currents. like a desert waiting for rain, i stalled at the sound
        of your name.

        poet writer chef

        korea kazakhstan sri lanka

        i'm not here nor there

        an eighth departing.

Natasha says we shouldn't heat our curries too high in the microwave

in case the airbnb house-lords upstairs get a whiff and kick
us out
or ask us to use deodorant
or make us out to be some sort of people who munch

but fuxk that i say

let that garlic sizzle, sis
let that fenugreek stew with green mangoes
let that turmeric leave stains like graffiti

we brought our own rice cooker
so we can do what we want

we wore our shoes in your hot tub
mixing jaggery in
we messed with your thermostat
set it to a tropical sunburst sunrise

we can do what we damn please
because this is our poem
about being on holiday
just try and catch us and
like free roaming stray dogs
we'll duck out stage right
whenever we like

she waved and i
for Maddison

she waved and i ...
dieeeeedd!
like melted or something
till there was
puddle me on the floor
m&b: mop and bucket

it's me,
coiling the vape
rounding off the bedposts
squeegees for hands

it's me,
the nine-minute egg
the tungsten cowboy
h&s: happy and sad

i've been
   , i mean
       i am
          tofu style: silken

Still cheers

my uncle doesn't keep a single knife
sharp in the house
my great regret is that
we never agreed on a consistent way of greeting each other
while i stick out my hand, he crumples my fingers
his belly going in for a hug

when i needed him the most, he was my found-blood
i brought him mandarins in hospital
after he tried to drive home mid-heart attack after school
and even though his stomach was an outside sack
we talked like we do, super-glued

my uncle, he streams boxing matches in bed
on a beat-up janky old website from the early 2000s
beside the pixelated boxing gloves, like red velvet bricks,
ads for fuxkme people pop out
and they're just there
lounging
like they own the place
sitting naked waiting in the lobby
while my uncle jumps through loopholes
chasing little x's around the screen

i go in for a hug with my shoulders and he
tilts his head round and
still cheers

Harbour

When I wake up one of my socks is still half on my foot and the blanket is scrunched up at the bottom of the bed with me sideways inside it. Big.

Last night was big. Maybe our biggest night yet. We sold out of the salmon with sorrel sauce by seven thirty and I had to do fuxkin' cartwheels to keep that dick politician from throwing a 'don't you know who I am' like he did last time and the time before that.

The way he comes in here on a Thursday all smug-like – drinking the cheapest shxt. Bitxh, I'm the one doing you a favour. I shouldn't have stayed out that late with Mickee after service. I shouldn't have talked all that shxt about Maycee. My skin is breaking out so bad this week and I don't know how to keep my make-up from smearing each time I wipe fryer fat from my forehead.

The sun's creeping up the curry leaf plant on the windowsill. I pin my sock to the floor and peel it off my foot. The olive colander in the kitchen that Nikité got me for my birthday looks great with peaches in it in this light.

I grind the last of the coffee beans and line the Chemex with a paper filter by turning it inside out. Just before the jug comes to a boil, I flick the switch and bounce on my toes. There is half a loaf of bread from the markets in a brown paper bag by the window and some Ossau-Iraty wrapped in beeswax cloth in the cold pantry.

As the coffee drips and the sourdough sizzles – butter bubbling in a cast iron pan, I pick up one of the peaches and inspect it in the morning light.

Its downy tuft glistens as I rub it against my bare hips. Soft furs float in the sunlight. I put my lips to its skin. It tickles my tongue. Oh, how joyously juicy I used to be with you in the sun.

Eating a peach in the sun i wonder

Ravi is lying on a mattress the colour of the forest floor
his thoughts are rambutan bobbing
suspended in the goo of dreams
there is no substance as versatile as suspense
the truth is   it's not the leaving that hurts
but the bagel   the car ride back
the 60 k speed limit
the miramar cutting
the truth is   my heart was breaking
and i was afraid to go there with you
how long has it been?

i'm doing okay but
i've been lying
mostly to myself
chewing with emphasis
these thoughts i can't shake

i put on a mask, machan
i put on a mask!
though in my head   my heart
i was still keeping score

i was   flapping eyelids
trying to get up off the ground

i've been telling job seekers   soften your language
so that your name   all fleshy and ripe
doesn't set off any alarms during   hiring tests
doesn't get stuck in the throat of   hiring managers

i've been using too many 'you shoulds' lately
instead of   you could
instead of telling them   how many times
i've secretly tried   bleaching my name too

i put on a mask, machan
once a sign of solidarity
now a sign of defiance

cucumbers are starting to drop
but butter's still expensive as fuxk

the transmitter in the distance
hmmm, tempting
the house tips towards it

the magnolias are making a mess on the ground
i turn to rot
rot, meet the dirt
dirt, meet the shovel

the truth is   i'm tired
writing cute little poems to please white people
it's time to bring out the warm jets

given the chance   i'd be
the accent you unlearned
the curly hairs between squished flesh and squished flesh

dark brown dodol is a difficult and time-consuming dish to prepare
this toffee-like sugar palm-based confection
If you refrigerate it   the coconut oil solidifies white

the truth   is this beautiful brown body   lugs wonderful
sweet leaf, blue meanie   come back
eating a peach in the sun   i wonder

Sadie
Lawrence

Like
Human
Girls
/ all we
have is
noise

(one month) Anniversary

We finish the dinner. We barefoot the grass.
The river below hisses and
above us
the night hushes it.

The chicken-wire woodwork engraves my knees
and you are one jacket poorer, enduring the chill.
Tonight, the world is a pearl
cradled in adolescent hands.
Tonight, this bridge is a virginal marriage bed;
we were the first to wrap ourselves in its black blanket,
        the first to shake off the incandescent lint.
I tell you that I want to know you as I know myself,
'for every thought of yours to first occur to me', and
we each reach for the other's hand in the same instant.

All of dawn unfolds at once,
and we sprint like competitive children
across the football field,
to our separate beds.

On Tidy Self-Injury

I discovered myself in the tree's elbow.
The roots underneath jutted from the soil –
earth's spinal ridges. The branches above
scraped the blue from the sky in self-defence.

My new wounds glistened; the blood
turned gold in the drowning sun.
While I had been bird-curved,
back hunched and shunning,
the deep afternoon had painted the playground
purple and ushered my sorry shadow away.

Summer fizzled
against the canine bite in the air.
Autumn would soon see me become a spectacle
to school children, taking innocence hostage;
this vulture would have to find another perch
on which to harvest its own rot.

A few weeks later, on my parents' balcony,
I mourned a cat-savaged sparrow.
It kept its entrails tucked politely inside.
I gave it one swift kick and it plummeted,
limp wings catching one last breeze:

There, I thought, *now it's flying.*
It's flying now.

'All that death, I find it very beautiful'
after Francis Bacon

There is a rich architecture of gory arches, spine and ribcage –
meat so cadmium red it transcends colour and becomes
    fact.
There is life reduced to its primal carnage; a baby is born
bloodied and screaming,   a life ends in parallel.
There are Christian symbols layered here: thorny crown, stigmata,
blood upon flesh upon blood.

  There are breasts laid bare. Reduced to torso,
   something totally female is crammed behind a gilded frame.
Under heaving bosom, there is muscle. Behind every quivering prick:
a butcher wanders his gristly Eden.

We are here,

the Sunday market. In sausage casings, the women parade
to the horizon-line shore. Around everyone,
                        flies.

Puppy

My love stands in the laundromat,
Sunday best with blistered hands.
Heaven is a slurry of wet fabric
at his feet, and he indoctrinates me.

In the childhood photos he is
a pale cherub, the picture of
fury. In the mirror
he is fierce still.

I won't apologise for being young.
I can't help that
love took me in its jaws
like a weary old dog

and carried me home.

Ode to the Autism Diagnosis Report

thank you, but
I've already had my baptism.
dribble like dewdrops into my hair,
saliva slung like pearls unstrung –
oh I'm familiar! children are bloodhounds
for unbelonging, they snuffled like
truffle-pigs over my buried spirit. they
tore it from the ground and aired it out,
dirty laundry on the line.

yes, the first realisation stings,
but all the ones that follow devour.
I was shedding my velvet, an obesity
of gore. I was building my ant farm
palace, maggot sandcastle township.
I live in the mourning of normalcy.
it lives in me.

All Teenagers are Tapestries

Pia tore a chasm in her palm
running from the cops. the classic
high school horror story: a misguided
stunt – paranoia parkour – sliding down the underpass.
she was a golden-haired Grand Canyon of carnage
on the park bench. she filled Sam's bucket
a third of the way with blood
while I held her up. we all shook
like tectonic plates –
like scared teenage girls.

at the hospital with Rose, they sewed her
with suture so tough it itched. afterwards,
I held her hand anyway,
telling her they used to stitch people up
with human hair (before plastic and nylon took over).
telling her, if we'd been born a couple hundred years earlier,
we'd all be tapestries, sewn up with the fibres
of one another.

now the scar splits her life line in two.
it marks the memory linear, coursing like
the carelessly tossed silver of a river in aerial.
there's a piece of black gravel still buried underneath
like a souvenir.

(girlhood is made of blood
and it blooms just the same) (it spills
down your thighs, stems from your nose)
(sharing like teenage girls

Girls Against Minimalism >:-)

let me be ur junkyard conversation piece, ur kitsch bitch on the mantel!
I promise to make the guests wary of ur taste if u promise to bubble-wrap
me on moving day even though I'm indelicate, dense as fuckkk. baby, I've
got youthful aggression! I embody the intention to scream! also I'm made
of lurid pastel plastic, or nineteen-fifties porcelain. I'm an object in an
autonomous way I've gained sentience!! am I the sad clown portrait of
ur dreams? am I ur forever girl? ur rotating ballerina with face-paint
a centimetre off my mould? hey, speaking of mould, wouldya look at my
velvet interior! u love me cause I'm too much and I love u cause u saved me.
I used to be haunted

but not now! Never again (I promise)!

Leaving Home

I am epiphany bathing
as much as the shower will allow;
stopping the plug with suctioned palms and
delivering amateur sermons to the cellar spiders.
My housewarming debut:

if there is an absence, it is a tangible thing
that lives, like cockroaches, in the depths of the pantry –
in food arranged by inexperienced lovers.
If there is independence, it is a stray
feeding on the plum carcasses
that stop the shed door shut.
If these are hands, then praying is second nature;
if they are not, the dusk feasts on my cold body,
jaws snapping like an impatient hound.
This is not growing up.
There must be an alien thing
deep in the chasms of me
that I am growing around.

Retainer

My childhood home now has a black fence
and a new TradeMe listing. My baby teeth
are still buried in the back garden there.

The new house is a semi-detached that
breathes with the same cadence as me.
It is both cold and warm. The boy I loved
when the orthodontist still had his hands
in my mouth
cooks me dinner. I chew it
with my straight teeth.

When I remove the plastic case cutting my gums
in the morning, there is a sudden painful
freedom; an ache and a tenderness
(synonymous
in the 7 a.m. stillness).

Whenever my dentist says
retainer,
my whole being is rushed towards
alertness. Like it has just heard its name.

In which a nosebleed wakes me up

There are four doors
in the shortest hallway
on earth. They open and slam
like haunted mouths.
They shift with breath
like a lover in bed:
they are alive but unaware of life.

When the day disturbs the doorknobs
it sends hair-thin strands of light across the walls
like panicked insects. There is a rock
under which we all writhe,
and
when met with sunlight
we mistake it for death.

I forget to close the curtains.
I awake drowning in blood,
but at least I awake.

heart pervert dodo bird

punished for approaching//
death through naivety, bowled under
the picnic bench that drips vandalism
my twelve-year-old smile
all cheeks and endearment

and he//
shining chubby puppy fat
freckled to hell and back,
the philosophy is:
shout fighting words
strike with blunt objects
the execution is:
swift but not painless
the apology never came

and he//
cult leader narcissist
angelic pit bull,
interval passes bloodless
but I go back to class
a knot of flesh ribbons

and he//
touches my cheek
calls me soft
scolds me like a parent

the childhood bully//
teaches you many useless things
= the scope of human shame
extends forever doing laps
around the school field
tripping over mary-jane feet

so here lies me//
extinct, detached
social anxiety disorder sertraline
seven years angrier
now I curse and scream and
kick

so if he hears howling in the night//
I hope he knows I'm close

[NIGHTMARE INTERMISSION]

i thought i told him to leave me alone pt. 1

                              [I had a dream about u]
[okay]
                              [u killed me again]
[lol]
                              [I burn in the church of u]
                              [u don't know what u did
                                    to me. I incubate ur
                              sickness. ur a rapist in my
                              nightmares. ur a romantic]
[you're the wound]
                              [I'll cut those freckles off
                              u haven't earned them!!]
[and the knife]
                              [but ur the salt! I'm the wound
                              and the knife but u are the
                                    salt. u eroded me,
                                    u gave me ur decay.
                                          I'm tired.
                                    sleep won't come]
[death is like sleep]
                                          [...]
                                    [fuck u vulture]
                              [I'm not dead yet, and ur circling
                                    is making me spiteful]
                                          [if I live
                                    you starve]

itithtlma pt. 2

my nightmares liberate him and
fulfil his every casting call.
a lover, a butcher, a rapist,
the childhood bully –
hatred itself,

stringing my guts up
like streamers. he carves me from marble,
he violates me with knives.
he kicks my teeth out and we lie in tulips
like romantics. I rot in his company
all over again! thank you, dreamland!

when I wake the air is thick with terror and
I am a conch shell
with the sound of a crimson sea inside.
I will hold his head under
and listen to him try to breathe
through my blood. One day
he will want to be silent

and I will pull the sound of his voice out of him

[RECOMMENCE]

Clumsy

We halted the paradox
of walking each other home

by renting a two-bedroom flat
and, since then,

I have forsaken elegance.
When I get over-excited

and pin your skin between my elbow and
the floor, you promise

to take it in your stride,
knowing that

when I was a child I let loose
in art galleries. Sprinting, cackling

like a gull, I ignored boundaries. Let my
fingers pester the brushstrokes.

Now I chase you,
tackle you to the ground

and kiss behind your ears,
into your palms. A brilliant truth:

I would sacrifice my beauty
before letting yours be untouched.

heartbreak (living next to the kindergarten)

it is a Thursday morning/
and I join the chorus of children
who believe they are being abandoned for
the final time/
the anger at being perceived as small
at odds with the knowledge that we are/
we sing with terror and howl with grief/
all we have is noise/
to push against our teeth/ we have
found our fists/ and the adults are concerned/
we've learned things we hate to know/
we are tiny pillars of sweat and tears///

screaming *BUT I LOVE YOU*
SO YOU CAN'T LEAVE ME

on being a creature

tied to a stake in the garden >
inside my body, the perpetual tantrum >
the bonnie beast, digging its fingers
into the ground > stability in its daily serving sizes
> growling at the overhead lights

[I envy pets
with not the vocabulary to know
what they are]

but sometimes my best friend comes over >
despite all the missed calls > and she wakes me up
to make 2 Minute Noodles and sit
outside the back door > holding a joint
like a teacup > pinky fingers out > real delicate >
like a human girl

God of Ugly Things / contemplations on shibari

I am still too young to clean the windows;
like a child, I believe the rain washes everything away.
now there's a wētā twitching and struggling
completely contorted in glimmering string,
shying from a spider. from where I sit,
staring on my bed,
it has the arch of a woman;
at twelve, I dizzied myself with
Japanese erotica gifs on Tumblr.
twisted
with rope, even the slenderest bodies
bulged. hung from the ceiling   like
    like   flies on tape. better restrained
where they could be seen and heard
struggle. they
were always pale – check –
and young – check – and strung
up like elegant meat, drying for a feast.
the spider lingers, rejoicing in its capacity
for violence. sympathy twitching,
I'm a victim by proximity again.

Earworm in B Minor

even when the world is silent,
i am not. there is so much noise
inside the body. sound landscape =
little sonic forest. those youtube videos
where they hook fungus up to a synthesiser.
voyeurs for the internal monologue of
death-sweet beings. i am
wretched

but catchy
in my gut gurglings. the full moon
of my cystic acne scar pulls the
gore tides of my stomach in
and out like stitches.
whatever lives under my tongue fizzes
i am harrowed by it, however

relieved to know I'm not hollow
but instead sloshing
with thick pink inhabitants

                    and
                  sometimes

i swear i can hear the mites
in my eyelashes sing
and fuck
and cry elegies to life
and curses to the life they live on

Thank God

for the breeding kink:

the earth will be repopulated
with It Girls in no time and
their glossed Dior lips will blow
New Bubblegum Moons and

we will build altars in cyberspace
and crypts in the cloud in preparation
for the romantic young deaths
we are hoping they'll have

they will really connect with *The Virgin
Suicides* 1999 directed by Sofia Coppola and
the scene in *Girl, Interrupted* where
Daisy kills herself

they are exquisite bitches
with precious little to do
but yawn awake in swathes of silk
in bodies like a fistful of baby birds
and be adored for a month or two

before stoking the flames of their own pyre
with their beech-tree limbs
########## winking

away #########

Leaving Home II
(or, the shadow that home casts)

I am standing in the shadow
that home casts,
trembling like a leaf and
haunted as graveyard dirt:
pushed aside –
packed into –

here, the cardboard box outside the back door
that sat for months
growing an ecosystem in the rain,
pushing roots and glowering,
sick with abandonment:
even when the landlord complained
you never picked it up.

here, the spot where the wind whistled
through the crack in the ceiling and
dampness flourished over the tile.
the things we took photos of as proof
before we moved in.

here, the passionfruit vine I trained
to climb the front porch.
in a metaphor too obvious
it withered and died,
drying to the texture of moth wings
the day I packed my boxes.

I was sitting in the shadow that
you cast,
chin crinkled like balled paper,
sick with abandonment and
you didn't pick me up.

haunted house, how dare you:
I can see ghosts
and I can see people
but I could never tell the difference.

Pet Name

I should've nicknamed you something
obscure: my little xylophone with your
ribcage exposed. I never thought to
worry that one day the word would be
said without connotation, meaning only
A Young Dog. What your mum calls to
the pets when she climbs the spiral
staircase from the garage to the lounge.
Just another family home I'll never see
again; one more place that flattened its
palm to stop cradling me. When the
word stops hurting you, I will feel a
seismic shift down my apple-core centre.
Is it selfish to want it to jolt forever?
Prick up your sensitive ears? Sting and
splinter, break your heart like the death
of something small and precious and
helpless? Puppy, pet name in the truest
sense, I always intend to be permanent.
Puppy, why was I the one to wait at the
door?

I'm not like other girls (I'm much worse)

I love you to death, baby –
so yours or mine?
You smoothed my hair
while I lapped at tap water,
taking my evening sertraline.

I shaved my eyebrows off in December
and dyed my hair in June. I started
wearing oversized shirts and became
dog shit on your dress shoes. Darling,
I eat Froot Loops with a shovel!
You said it yourself,
I'm wasting a skinny frame!
I'm beautiful but unattractive!

But did you think it through? The sunset
followed us home and cast your shadow thin:
I was twisting the engagement ring,
I was telling anyone that would listen.
You had that nap while I was howling,
weeping in the next room.
Was it when you sunk your teeth in
that you first realised?
Dearest, did you think I wouldn't be tough?

Baby, darling, dearest,
I love you to death but, damn,
looks like I bled out while you were away!
Your eyesight was shit. I stepped on your glasses.
Hindsight's a bitch but she's nothing compared to me:
I've got skinned knees and freckles
like a kid!
I've got hair on my legs for winter
(oh I keep myself warm)!

All that to say,
if heaven really was at your feet
I still wouldn't kneel for ya.

Winter

I am in the dark, pouring boiling water
into a narrow opening
I am having my throat slit super slowly
I am putting the O in holy:
I am opening my mouth very wide

I am running my hand under the cold tap
I am alone and sizzling
I am alive,
hence the blistering

Aphantasia

I want to stay forever at my mother's table
describing the parts of the world that aren't
immediate. Remind her of the porchlight,
like an ugly moon,
pooling over the balcony of the childhood home.

How the silhouettes of dead moths ached like craters
against the LED
and the egg yolk of the night slipped
down the back of our necks with a chill.
She held her arms up to the night sky like
a chalice to be filled.

I will make her recall the rosebud fist
of the happiest baby in the hospital,
orange robes like a mandarin rind and underneath
tiny, pale and pink. Hong Kong humidity flushed her
ripe and took her home, already having learned
to smile.

I will say
the memory of beautiful things is just as important
as the image. This is hypocrisy:
I will not say *I'm so glad my mind has eyes*
I'm so glad to have you forever.

Conclusion

> Hi.
> I am calling to tell you that the cicadas
 are ripening fit to burst around here +

( )

> it's the part of summer where the citronella candle
starts to Almost Work
> I used to attend bonfires this time of year +
go to house parties and ask for the 'girl drinks'
until somebody handed me a vodka cruiser
> and nobody else thought that was funny

( )

> sorry, do you hear that?
the earth is purring like a cat +
the electricity in here is so loud
> the weather is good and golden
I am exhausted
> but laughing +
with my head removed from the sand

( )

> how about I live with you and Rose next year? +
we can mount those plates on the wall
> the heartache made me up my meds so
you can finally take me to Wellington clubs +
I can be a chaos of grief in a sexy way this time

( )

> we were by the hot tub +
both of you had scissors,
each delegated a half of my head
> you cut me that mullet
> you always watch me become myself

( )

> I'll be the mould in your tapestry
if you'll be the threads in mine +
delicious It Girls in the daylight
sewing each other up
> we very nearly made our exes feminists!
> we must be doing something right +
if not, we'll get 'em next time!

( )

> it was last summer
> we were eating fish and chips +
you watched me hit a mosquito off my arm
and stare at the blood +
> yes, it was for the reason you thought.
Sorry #

Notes

Pukapuka mapi / Atlas
'A Room Recording', 'Scurvy Girls' and 'Taranaki' were all first published in *Starling*.
'Celesta' and 'Tataraimaka Pā' first appeared in *a fine line*.
'Ōākura Beach' was first published in *Poetry New Zealand Yearbook*.
'Tataraimaka Pā' and 'Ōākura Beach' have appeared in *Pūhia*.

Favourite Flavour House
'Six a.m. in Colombo / Cinnamon Gardens' first appeared in 'The Friday Poem'
    at *The Spinoff*, 8 September 2023.
A version of 'To find your heroes are shit dancers' appeared in 'The Friday Poem'
    at *The Spinoff*, 1 April 2022.

Like Human Girls / all we have is noise
An earlier version of 'Earworm in B Minor' was published in *Overcom: Celebrate*
    for International Asexuality Day.

Tessa Keenan (Te Ātiawa) is from Taranaki and is now based in Te Whanganui-a-Tara. She would like to thank her whānau, partner, friends and tūpuna for the constant inspiration and support during the writing of her chapbook. Her poems have appeared in *Starling, a fine line, Poetry Aotearoa Yearbook* and *Pūhia*.

romesh dissanayake is a writer from Te Whanganui-a-Tara Wellington. His work has appeared in *The Spinoff, The Pantograph Punch, Enjoy Contemporary Art Space* and *A Clear Dawn: New Asian Voices from Aotearoa New Zealand* (edited by Paula Morris and Alison Wong). His first novel, *When I open the shop*, was the winner of the 2022 Modern Letters Fiction Prize and is forthcoming from THWUP in 2024.

Sadie Lawrence is an undergraduate student of creative writing and media studies. *Like Human Girls / all we have is noise* was written from ages seventeen to nineteen. Her autism screening was inconclusive.

First published 2024
Auckland University Press
Waipapa Taumata Rau
University of Auckland
Private Bag 92019
Auckland 1142
New Zealand
www.aucklanduniversitypress.co.nz

ISBN 978 1 77671 123 9

Published with the assistance of Creative New Zealand

A catalogue record for this book is available from the National Library
of New Zealand

Design by Greg Simpson
This book was printed on FSC® certified paper
Printed in Singapore by Markono Print Media Pte Ltd